Believe
in yourself
— & —
you will be
Unstoppable

iUniverse books may be ordered through booksellers or by contacting:

iUniverse
1663 Liberty Drive
Bloomington, IN 47403
www.iuniverse.com
844-349-9409

Because of the dynamic nature of the Internet, any web addresses or links contained in this book may have changed since publication and may no longer be valid. The views expressed in this work are solely those of the author and do not necessarily reflect the views of the publisher, and the publisher hereby disclaims any responsibility for them.

Any people depicted in stock imagery provided by Getty Images are models, and such images are being used for illustrative purposes only.
Certain stock imagery © Getty Images.

Scripture quotations are from the Holy Bible, King James Version (Authorized Version). First published in 1611. Quoted from the KJV Classic Reference Bible, Copyright © 1983 by The Zondervan Corporation.

ISBN: 978-1-6632-4256-3 (sc)
ISBN: 978-1-6632-4257-0 (e)

Library of Congress Control Number: 2022913159

Print information available on the last page.

iUniverse rev. date: 07/29/2022

PRC

PERSEVERANCE, RESILIENCE & COURAGE WITH GRACE

WAVENEY BLACKMAN

A C K N O W L E D G M E N T S

Many thanks to Almighty God for inspiring and blessing me with wisdom, long life and insight, without which I could not have completed this book.

It is true that no great work is ever accomplished without active or passive support from the people with whom we are surrounded.

Like all labors of love, writing a book is harder than I thought but more rewarding than I could have ever imagined. Thus, it is not difficult to conclude, that this motivational manifesto would not have been possible without their help, keen insight, and ongoing support. I would like to express my gratitude and appreciation to all those who encouraged the writing of this motivational manifesto.

To my niece Dr. Jacque Colbert, thanks for the foreword you contributed. The veracity of the foreword reminds me of my purpose, to help others in finding a healthy, positive approach to living their best life through realistic, practical actions for success.

Many thanks to Ms. Elnora Andries for her valuable assistance and encouragement in the completion of this motivational manifesto. The numerous times she sat with me as I wrote, allowing me to feel free to verbalize my thoughts and ideas, utilizing her as my sounding board, giving affirmation with a nod of her head, while making corrections when proof reading.

Ms. Faye Bobb-Semple, my dear cousin, who I called on frequently to proof read my writings, and provide positive feedback. Faye, you sat with me when the idea of writing this motivational manifesto started from a concept in my head. You continued to strengthen me with prayers, love and encouragement; always showing interest in the progress of my writings.

To my two children, Cleon and Charlene, especially my son, Cleon for always being the person I could turn to during those moments of writer's block. Your support sustained me in ways that I never realized I needed. Your gift of making light of issues is a gift to me. I found at the end of many of our conversations, we are both laughing at life. To my grandchildren, Khaylayah, Eli and Connor, thanks for letting me know that you have nothing but great memories of me. I am so thankful to have you all in my life. To my special angel "Clay," thank you for being my first inspiration.

Special thanks to the dedicated team at iUniverse Publishers, particularly Mr. Buddy Dow and Ms. Leigh Allen. Mr. Dow, it is appropriate in my opinion, to single you out for your extraordinary support during the challenging process of my writing this motivational manifesto. I trust and respect your professional demeanor, being a non-judgmental listener. You created a business-friendly platform for me to speak openly...and then you followed through to get the job done.

Barbara Dickson-Carter, you are always checking in on my progress, cheering and encouraging me to stay the course. Thanks for giving me the push I needed during the times when I felt tired, reminding me that I am good at providing motivation and opportunities for others.

Dr. Tanisha Kadiri, you believed in me, stretching me to go to new levels with my work. You consistently encouraged me with relevant inspirational quotes, reminding me that I was born for such a time as this, convincing me that there are individuals out there in the world that need PRC. Thank you Dr. Kadiri.

Finally, to all others that have been a part of this journey, thank you!

F O R E W O R D

Living a life of Perseverance, Resilience, and Courage, never happens overnight. Each character trait can only be built and refined by one's lived experience, and Waveney Blackman has done just that. She didn't wish for it, she worked for it! Waveney has truly lived PRC; Perseverance, Resilience, and Courage and you will experience it as you turn each page of this book. With this monograph/manifesto, Waveney has written from the heart with conviction and grace. She's masterfully curated a practical guide with salient examples that are applicable to anyone who may have taken a wrong turn or been thrown a curveball. This manifesto underscores Waveney's personal story which serves as the backdrop of how she was compelled to share what it truly means to be down but *NEVER* out.

Waveney has lived a life that consistently illustrates the need to go above and beyond with grit, grace, and courage. Along the way, she stepped into unchartered waters with great faith and a conviction to succeed. Although this book is written with a focus, on women who in their quest to reach the success that had generational benefits for their families, faltered or made missteps, its chronicled stories allow any reader to find wisdom in the pages. Waveney carefully lays out what it takes to have a winner's mindset no matter one's station in life. While many have written from a theoretical perspective, Waveney trumps it all with her lived experiences; and in so doing, makes this manifesto a true game-changer.

Dr. Jacque Colbert, D.M
Global HR Executive, Google

INTRODUCTION

'But they that wait upon the Lord shall renew their strength;
they shall mount up with wings as eagles; they shall run, and not be weary; and they shall walk, and not faint.'

Isaiah 40:31

I have used this image of the eagle to symbolize vision, manifestation, perseverance, resilience, and courage.. The eagle is the spark that ignited the dormant flame in me and energized my thoughts, goals, and vision to become my best self. I decided to recalibrate and reset my life after the negative experiences that had brought me to that point.

In self-reflection, 2018, 2019, and 2020 were transformative years for me. Those years of adversity afforded me the opportunity to reach deep into the core of my being and awaken my spiritual, emotional, and mental energy that lay stagnant. I quickly realized that I should not just *survive*. I must *thrive*. I then revisited the path that had brought me to that point. Many thoughts crossed my mind. I have always been unconventional, taking the road less traveled. Many of my choices led me in directions different from most. I have stepped into uncharted waters with faith and conviction to succeed.

I experienced betrayal and deception that contributed to my demise while I was still recovering from the accidental, horrific automobile death of my only grandson (at the time). I had worked very hard to establish a successful business. I became very ill and had to be away for a while, leaving important decisions in the hands of persons who I subsequently discovered did not have my best interests at heart. I was duped!

It was then that I realized what my mother meant when she often said to me, "Waveney, you are too trusting. You trust people too much." I came to the realization that my mother was correct. My trusting nature became my Achilles' heel. I have learned that you have to be careful with the people with whom you surround yourself. The eagle reminds me that soaring above gives you a clear perspective of the intentions of others.

It has been said that hindsight is 20/20. That is true. Having gone through that traumatic experience from misguided choices, I have learned valuable lessons. Time is never lost. Adversity introduces you to your true self. You can use every experience as a teacher. We can use the rocks thrown at us as stepping-stones to become our better selves. Coupled with my innate gifts to motivate, inspire, and mentor, the prescription was written; PRC was born!

As I focus on this new journey, coupled with the fact that I have always been an effective mentor and a certified coach, I am convinced that this motivational manifesto will help any individual faced with unforeseen catastrophic circumstances to believe in themselves, recalibrate and reset their lives, and become better versions of themselves. Everyone who reads this motivational manifesto will benefit and find PRC to be a game changer. It is tried-and-true. I wrote this motivational manifesto from a practical perspective, hoping I can positively influence the lives of others. I applied these principles and have successfully regained my steps, living my best life.

I therefore created this motivational manifesto with the desire to help the reader foster change, increase life's stability, and thrive in any situation, with Perseverance, Resilience, and Courage (PRC) with grace. I have witnessed the positive results of this prescription. I know starting all over again takes courage, but believe that success is possible when you are faced with challenges, and you can triumph with Perseverance, Resilience, and Courage as your companions. Unblur your mind, and become great!

It took these three words—(1) *Perseverance*, (2) *Resilience*, and (3) *Courage* (PRC)—to place me on the path to becoming the best version of myself. God blesses each human with a gift. We just have to take the time to do the soul-searching and self-reflection to find our purpose and passion. It is written in Proverbs 18:16, "Our gifts will make way for us." My life is a message of hope and new beginnings, and it is my prayer that you will find this motivational manifesto inspiring, motivating, and fulfilling!

1

Be the Architect of Your Own Life—Carve It in Excellence

For I know the plans I have for you, "declares the Lord", plans to prosper you and not to harm you, plans to give you hope and a future.

Jeremiah 29:11

Welcome to "Riding the waves to becoming your best self." Let's embrace this journey as we endeavor to live our best life. This motivational manifesto I share with you provides a step-by-step prescription for successful outcomes.

"How can I become the architect of my own life, *again*?" I asked. I, like others, did not believe it was possible for me to create a new blueprint for carving my life in excellence. I had worked hard in the past and reached the heights of success, I thought, and everything had come tumbling down. Life at times became overwhelmingly challenging, as the daunting thought of starting all over again depressed me. I was petrified about my future and completely paralyzed by fears, especially fear of financial insecurity.

I felt safe in this cocoon I created, nursing the victim mindset. The cocoon defined my identity and allowed me to exist as a person. Thankfully, this self-pity did not work very long for me. I realized that this was not the life I wanted for myself, so I flipped the coin and changed my perspective. I fervently started praying again. I stopped dwelling on the past, forgiving myself and others for misguided choices, understanding why I was in this situation and the reasons why I was seeking change. Here are some questions I asked myself.

- "What got me to my current situation?"
- "How can I calibrate a new path for a new successful experience?"
- "What else am I good at creating or developing?"

Transforming my life was not easy, but it was worth the effort. With dedicated motivation, I made progress. Before long, my entire mindset shifted. I managed to reconnect with my lost enthusiasm for life, and even better, every day, I was finding more opportunities to smile, connect, share, and be happy (with purpose). You have to take action. Believe you can, and you will.

In my personal and professional experience, becoming the architect of my life required, first deciding that I am capable of creating my own life circumstances. Fear and doubt were soon replaced by hope, and life became a vast field of possibilities. I found a new sense of peace, being accepting of the things I had no power over, and at the same time being courageous enough to change what I could.

I recalibrated my path with a new mindset and determination, believing in myself, reminding myself there are always setbacks in life. Things hardly ever go according to plan, and sometimes, there is nothing we can do about it.

Being the architect of your own life can isolate you, prevent you from further development, or liberate you in the world you create. It can evoke your senses and provide you with limitless inspiration.

We are the architects of our own lives. With every goal we set and every choice we make, we are in essence drawing the floor plan of the dream life we want to build or rebuild. As we take action and move ahead to accomplish the goals we set, we are creating the life we envision.

In this book, you will find inspirational and motivational quotes to encourage you as you persevere with resilience and courage. These applied principles have indeed changed my life and the lives of many others who have followed PRC's prescription.

Whatever your spiritual or religious beliefs, one thing is certain: you only live once. How we live this gift called *life* is up to each of us. The better we do in setting our goals today, and having a vision of what we want our future to be, the more beautiful and satisfying our life will become.

The first part of becoming the architect of your life is deciding that you are capable of creating your life circumstances. I believe that every person has the ability to be the architect of their life, or they should. Is it always going to be easy? No! The best way to predict your future is to create it.

If you want to master your life, you need to learn how to overcome adversity and hard times. Keep going; everything you need will come to you at a perfect time. You have to tell the world who you are; if you don't know, the world will tell you. At any given time, you have the power to say, "This is not how my story ends. I did then what I thought I knew; now that I know better, I shall do better!"

How do I know? I have faced some big challenges in my life that have tested my faith and strength. By deciding to make the choice to pick myself up and push forward, I realized that I was the only one responsible for my peace of mind and destiny. The manner in which I responded and chose to react mattered.

You will master your life only when you master your thoughts. Do not be afraid to start over, or better yet, continue working on your dreams to rebuild what you want. I was once told that you have to accept responsibility for the results you get in life; when you understand your *why* behind anything you do, you become better equipped to make empowered decisions. It is then that you take back the power to change your future. This is your life. You get to decide what success looks like for you.

I personally feel, and hope you do too, that we should make the best of life. We should strive to live our best life, not just *survive*. I am talking about *self-actualization*, visualizing all that you want from life and making it a reality. Carve your own life in excellence!

Know what you want, visualize it, and create it in your life. Is it always going to be easy? Not really … but if living your best life while becoming your best self is important to you, then riding the waves will be an exciting journey. Let's begin!

Success is no accident. It is intentional, coupled with hard work, Perseverance, Resilience, and Courage: PRC. Practice being aware of your thoughts, words, and actions. This mindset will help you better create a life of your choosing. Determine what you want and why you want it. Once you understand what is important to you, you can pursue your passions and achieve anything. What you become by achieving your goal is much more rewarding than actually reaching the goal. Be your own best advocate. Life is about creating yourself, not finding yourself.

Your goal must always be to become better than you were before. Never compete with someone else; never opt to be mediocre; never just daydream and wish. Be passionate and excited about goals and plans to succeed. Keep in mind you cannot change your destination overnight, but you can change your direction overnight. Your goals should be your compass or GPS that guides you along while showing you the possibilities of your journey's choices and roadblocks. Recalibrate when necessary!

I created a vision board for the positive things I wanted to attract in my life while manifesting them, believing that I was the architect of my reality. I expanded my awareness and orchestrated the evolution of my consciousness to choose. I reminded myself that I am powerful and can create the life I deserve!

I started spending time alone in meditation with my higher power to recollect my thoughts and set new life priorities. I refused to waste time focusing on others' achievements and successes. I visualized the achievement of my dreams. I simulated the successful life I wanted in my head, reminding myself that the power of thought is very mighty while motivating myself to become my best self.

This renewed thinking worked for me! If you believe and take action, you have the ability to create the life you envision, once you are willing to do the hard work.

I know many things in life are beyond our control, but stay focused. Do not give up; keep moving in the right direction. Remember the only person you are destined to become is the person you decide to be!

When you are truly the architect of your life, your life can be anything you want. It is up to you. Your destiny lies in your hands, and you can be successful if you will it, and work it. Carving our lives in excellence is the blueprint that takes us to success, yielding great rewards. Circumstances may slow us down, but they cannot stop us once we demonstrate Perseverance, Resilience, and Courage! We only live once. The choice is ours, and it has always been!

As I write this chapter, I am in real time sharing inspirational, encouraging words and thoughts with my teenage granddaughter. This page is dedicated to her. I am writing exactly what I told her with the hope that this will inspire and encourage her and every reader, regardless of age.

Be kind and thankful; always remember to show gratitude. Pray every day, acknowledging your highest power. Respect yourself and others. Love yourself; know you are worthy of being loved. Self-care is important. Think positively. Education is vital to living your best life. Make decisions that affect your future, not your feelings. You are created by the hand of God for a purpose. You are an unrepeatable miracle that must make good choices regarding your dream of becoming great in life.

This is your life; you get to decide what success looks like for you. *Dream big.* Have a sense of greatness. It has been said that if you can dream it, you can do it. I believe that! For a dream to become a reality, you have to see it in your mind; see its fulfillment, whatever it may be. Never give up. Do not let the negatives of life control you. Rise above them. Use them as your stepping-stones!

Let your daily mantra be "I will live and build the life I am proud to live." Be still. Be present. Be mindful! You are enough.

We are not monolithic. Surround yourself with positive dreamers and doers, believers and thinkers, and those who see the potential in you even when you do not see it yourself. *Be the architect of your life; carve it in excellence!*

You must have control
of the authorship of your
own destiny; place your
future in good
hands ... your own!
The pen that writes your
life story must be held in
your own hand.

PERSEVERANCE, RESILIENCE & COURAGE WITH GRACE

Reflections

Was this chapter insightful or inspiring?

Your thoughts:

CHAPTER
2
PRC Explained

Let Us Run With Perseverance
The Race Marked Out For Us.
Hebrews 12:1

P Is for *Perseverance*

It has been my experience that perseverance is the ember of success. Even when trauma, hardship, and despair have blown out the fire, the spark keeps hope alive; the ember remains warm, igniting the will to muster the strength to attempt to begin again, and again, and again! And when you succeed, you will hear the whisper saying, "I knew I could do it." I have an inspirational picture framed in my office that says, "She thought she could and she did!"

We all have heard many times before that perseverance is the key to success, but we may have never really stepped back and thought about what *perseverance* actually means and how it is relevant to our lives. We get bogged down by little failures and just give up on dreams long cherished. It takes determination, perseverance, and fortitude for anyone to be successful.

Failures are sometimes mostly beneficial in that they provide the people who erred with new experiences or knowledge so they know how to perform well or better in the future. This allows the people to persevere. When you fail at anything, learn from it and keep moving forward. Failure isn't meant to give you a reason to quit; it is meant to show you a different way to approach your goal. Do not stop when obstacles arise. Persist and trust yourself and your vision until you have what you need to accomplish your dreams.

In my experience, we humans are capable of achieving lots of things with perseverance, hard work, and belief in ourselves. The greater the challenges I have faced in the past, the harder I have had to work to overcome them, proving to myself that I am capable.

One of my favorite writers, John C. Maxwell, has said that "perseverance draws sweetness out of adversity. The trials and pressures of life and how we face them define us." Persevering means doing something steadfastly despite difficulty or delay in achieving success. Do not give up too soon, and if you fail, try once more. Keep trying as many times as it takes, if it is worthwhile for you.

Babies do not give up every time they fall when learning to walk. They pick themselves up and try again with encouragement and support, repeating the process despite the bruises and bumps along the way. It never occurs to the babies that they might fail. They never stop trying until they are walking, running, and laughing happily.

Now, what about you—do you give up too soon and too often? How many times have you pulled yourself back up when you got bumped and bruised from life's obstacles? Do not self-sabotage. Most of us are guilty of this at one time or another. It all starts with our thinking. Thoughts of fear, doubt, and failure begin to invade our thinking. Keep in mind that perseverance is the foundation of great achievers, coupled with determination, which can be found in every walk of life and every age. We succeed because we are determined to succeed.

Perseverance is an essential human virtue. When one continuously tries something, one will, eventually, succeed. When success arrives, there also comes with it the pride of not giving up, learning from errors along the way, and finally succeeding. We all need a healthy balance of proper goals and perseverance to see us through!

Do not give up!

Challenges are what make life interesting and overcoming them is what makes life meaningful.

R Is for *Resilience*

Have you ever wondered why some people remain calm in the face of adversity while others crumble? People who are able to effectively navigate the highs and lows of life have what is known as *resilience*, an ability to bounce back from adversity. It is less about who you are and more about how you think.

Whenever you come across a difficult situation, you have two choices: you can either (1) let your emotions get the best of you and become paralyzed by doubt or (2) lift yourself up from the negative and transform pain into possibility. Resilience is a process that builds up over time through experiences that encourage you to overcome adversity. It is an opportunity to build self-esteem and self-determination. By developing coping strategies, you enable yourself to become mentally stronger.

To appreciate success, you have to experience and overcome failure. In fact, very few successful people were spared from facing difficult challenges. Even if you consider yourself to be problem-free—someone with very little negative experience—you will inevitably encounter some challenges at some point along your life's journey. These experiences may bend you, but they do not have to break you. It is imperative that we learn to successfully navigate our way through tough times.

In essence, resilient individuals possess the ability to overcome misfortune and recover. With a resilient mindset, a business reversal or personal setback will often bring out the best in you, enabling you to find courage and strength you never knew you possessed.

As I write, I am reminded of a woman who fought many battles and is still standing; cried many tears and is still smiling; and has been broken, betrayed, abandoned, and rejected but still walks proudly, laughs loudly, lives without fear, and loves without doubt. This woman is beautiful, and humble … this woman is me!

Each of us has the power to develop a resilient mindset. Like a muscle, it needs to be conditioned and strengthened frequently. Sometimes, we have to hit our emotional threshold before we are able to tap into our personal resilience.

Resilience is knowing that you are the *only one* who has the power and the responsibility to pick yourself up. It is accepting your new reality and whether you recharge or endure. Do not get frustrated or disappointed. Resilience starts with having the desire to change internally. Do not develop a victim mentality. Take personal responsibility for your life. Resilient people look at a problem and ask, "What is this trying to teach me?" Make time to reflect and rest. Ignore doubters and naysayers, especially if they are in your head. Continually nudge your comfort zone, and refuse to live a life of mediocrity. Choose intentionally!

When we intentionally choose to be resilient, we can change things, even if we do not completely eradicate them. We can negate genetic factors, early life experiences, and the effects of catastrophic experiences by deciding on a positive path, while focusing on and working toward productive goals. We can totally alter our situations.

In my experience, the road to success is sometimes paved with some failures. Failure is a normal part of life. You cannot build resilience unless you are mentally and emotionally challenged. Access your internal GPS and recalibrate your path. In the end, we may all become more than we expected as we explore a different route. We must be prepared to ride the waves of life on the journey to becoming our best selves. Just simply change directions, and keep going in the direction of the life you were born to live. We have the power to truly change things. Remember Jeremiah 29:11.

"Be Strong And Of Good Courage; Do Not Be Afraid, Nor Be Dismayed, For The Lord Your God Is With You Whereever You Go".

Joshua 1:9

C Is for *Courage*

The symbol of the lion represents courage and personal strength, among other attributes. Courage is often associated with the lion. The lioness takes care of her cub or cubs as we should take care of each other. Lions take pride in family and love for each other.

Nine years ago, I thought my life was good. My children and only grandchild (at that time) brought sunshine to my life that I thought could never be dimmed. Then suddenly, without warning, things changed. My dear and only grandson died in a horrific car accident, leaving behind two children, at the tender ages of three years and two years, without a father. Was this life-changing? Absolutely!

Subsequently, the business I had spent time building, inspiring and motivating others to do the same, closed. My life as I knew it fell apart.

Life isn't easy. Whether it is good or bad, it is all part of the journey. It presents experiences and lessons from which we draw strength and on which we build to help us in our future endeavors. There isn't a handbook, that I know of, that warns us of specific circumstances and pain we may face, but there is a solution: Perseverance, Resilience, and Courage (PRC). You must find courage to overcome unforeseen circumstances, instead of falling prey to your journey difficulties.

I realized that there comes a time when you have to accept these facts of life: trauma, pain, and negative situations that leave deep scars across your heart. But that doesn't mean those things should hold you back. After all, there will be more hurdles to jump. How you decide to handle the situations is what will make the difference in your future—courage!

We all have decisions to make in life—some big, some small—but the decision that outweighs them all is whether we choose to go BIG (believe in God). When we make this decision, everything else becomes possible; all dreams are attainable. I challenge you all, don't settle for the small things in life, but strive for BIG with courage.

Do not focus on failures or disappointments; do not become discouraged in moving forward. Courageously look at the presented challenges as opportunities to improve yourself and help others. Buoyed by optimism and enthusiasm, I motivate myself to look for meaning in my life-altering circumstances. From my pain, I found the courage to pick myself up and recalibrate my path while asking, "What is the lesson to be learned here?" I experienced grace under pressure, reminding myself that every person faces different challenges during their day-to-day life, while feeling that inner courage, daring to go on. To be able to get through each day and not give up, while meeting the challenges of life, is also the definition of being courageous.

I have definitely had my share of experience overcoming adversity. Each time I encountered a new situation that seemed completely devastating, I reflected on the strength that was born inside me out of the very pain I was experiencing.

I have grown to learn that you must have faith in yourself. Faith is required when overcoming adversity. Believe you can do anything by reminding yourself, "I am going to overcome this." Your state of mind is more important than the situation because that is where courage, strength, and resilience are born.

Understand that whatever experience you face is part of life, and it won't be the first or last. Use your emotions to cultivate a stronger version of yourself. *Courage* is the power of the mind to overcome negative thoughts.

Courage, I feel, is a must if you are going to achieve the desires of your life. Without resilience and courage, the opportunity to succeed lessens because you do not have the ability to persevere.

It comes down to
perseverance and resilience
partnered with courage to
accomplish your goals.
Perseverance is overcoming
difficulties in spite of obstacles
or discouragement. Resilience is
never giving up even when
things get hard, bouncing back
from adversity with more
determination. Courage is to try
again and again, until you
succeed; dare to live the life
you have imagined!

PERSEVERANCE, RESILIENCE & COURAGE WITH GRACE

Reflections

Was this chapter insightful or inspiring?

Your thoughts:

CHAPTER

3

Vision

Vision

"Write the Vision and make it plain on tablets,

That he may run who reads it."

Habakkuk 2:2

Write the vision down that God places on your heart so that the goals are clear!

Visualize your highest self, and start showing up as that self. A *vision* is the most powerful and unique asset you have. Your vision has to be at the core of everything you do. It is unbelievable how powerful you can be when you have a clear vision. "Where there is no vision, the people perish" (Proverbs 29:18).

A clear vision, supported by definite plans, gives you a tremendous feeling of confidence and personal power. It has been my experience that the only person you are destined to become is the person you envision yourself to be. I was once part of a direct selling group, the manager of which insisted that we all repeat, "If it is to be, it is up to me," at the beginning of our sales meetings.

Having the vision of an eagle and the heart of a lion is a powerful combination to help ensure success. Do not let others limit your vision by telling you what you can't do. Speak what you seek until you see what you speak. Each day of my life, I have come to realise that people are as good as they are relevant to their family and the world at large. Your story is told from the evident change in your life's journey, which is a result from your vision and goals.

We are responsible for our happiness and success in most situations. In fact, we create and attract them. We must manifest them—through vision. We are the architects of our reality. We must choose our thoughts, our perceptions, and our reactions to external forces. We possess all the tools needed to expand our awareness, to orchestrate the evolution of our consciousness to choose to live our best life. Humans are that powerful.

When you see your vision, you will step into your destiny. Let us create the life we deserve. Visualize—write down your dreams and imaginations for the best life you want. But vision is not enough; it must be coupled with action and movement toward what we envision.

Having a vision allows you to create alignment in your life and to make choices for your life much more easily. It allows you to align your goals, relationships, and behavior while providing you with a clear direction. Your life's vision defines who you want to be and accomplishments for which you aim. Your vision helps define the goals by giving you a framework to evaluate those goals.

Your vision becomes your why, answering questions like:

- "What sort of life do I want to live in comparison to the life I now live?"
- "What would bring more joy and happiness in my life?"
- "What are my values?"
- "What qualities do I want to develop?"
- "What would I most like to accomplish within a certain time frame?"
- "What kind of legacy would I like to leave behind?"

It will be helpful to write your thoughts and dreams down in a journal or create a vision board. Write the things that you are hoping to become or achieve. This will give you clues as to your vision for a better life. Describe your ideal life in detail. Allow yourself to dream and imagine … create a vivid picture in your head … *visualize*. If you find it difficult to envision your life for a long period, start with short-term goals, maybe three to five years into the future. This will give you a direction to move toward. You may want to set your writings aside for a while and revisit them from time to time to see whether you have changed your mind about anything.

It is important that I point out there is a difference between a vision and goals. *Goals* are individual experiences and accomplishments you strive for. A *vision* is the bigger picture. Your life's vision defines who you want to be known as and the accomplishments for which you aim. It defines the goals by giving you a framework to evaluate those goals. In the next chapter, we will talk more about goals and purposes.

In my earlier years, I did not quite understand what a vision entailed, but I knew in my head the following thoughts or dreams played significant roles in shaping the person I am.

- The type of life I want to live at a certain age
- The kinds of people with whom I want to be surrounded
- The greatest things I should be able to accomplish
- The kind of family I want to create
- What legacy I want to have when I die

Through experience, I have come to realize that I was able to improve my life by changing my plans, revisiting my initial goals and recalibrating a new path. I envisioned and created a new blueprint for a realistic, successful life. To summarize it all, your purpose explains what you are doing with your life, your vision explains how you are living your purpose, and your goals enable you to realize your vision.

To create your life's vision, you need to first identify what matters in life. This is where that philosophy class should come in handy— understanding the real meaning of life. How should you live your life? Your answer to "What matters in life?" won't be perfect, and that's fine. The point is to put a stake in the ground to work toward, and you can change your answer whenever you review your life's vision.

Craft a statement that describes what your ideal life looks like. This exercise can be fun and rewarding. Your vision statement should consist of an overall description of your ideal life, including a list of areas that matter most to you and your goals for each area.

Once you follow this exercise, you will likely see some benefits, as your vision will play in your mind as you unconsciously work toward it. Next, have a system where you regularly review your vision and goals and update your action plan for accomplishing those goals. A vision board can help with this.

What Is a Vision Board, and What Are Its Benefits?

A *vision board* is a collage of images, words, and quotes that represent your wishes or goals; it is intended to serve as an inspiration or motivation. It represents the life you hope to live in the future. You can also refer to it as your *dream board*. It is a tangible representation of the vision you have for yourself, helping you visualize your goals and achieve your dreams by harnessing the law of attraction. Vision boards can be incredibly powerful manifesting tools.

The more you surround yourself, and your mind, with the things you want to experience, the more you will actually get to experience those things in your life. I strongly believe that where your interest and purpose reside, your attention will be focused. " Think positive at all times!

A number of highly successful people have claimed vision boards were an important tool for their success. A vision board is usually constructed with a large piece of cardboard and a collage of different pictures and notes of wants, desires, needs, and dreams you wish to fulfill. You can hang it up on your bedroom wall as a reminder of the possibilities that you can realize. This is a great way to reinforce the vision and direction in your mind so that you can be surer of reaching your dreams.

When you continue to give your attention to the things you want, and you have a visualization of them, you will attract those things in your life, and an ideal life can become your reality. This relates to the concept of positive affirmations as well. However, just be careful because the Universe responds with both positive and negative. A negative example is if you look for reasons to support why you are having a bad day or are unhappy, then you will keep attracting annoyances or occurrences to prove you right.

Your vision board should be a flexible and fluid representation of your desires as they shift and morph throughout your life. In fact, it is recommended that you create a completely new vision board every six to twelve months to ensure it is up-to-date with your values and priorities.

I would recommend making this a fun event. Gather some of your best friends and some family members so you can all work on your own boards, dreams, and goals. Look through magazines, and cut out pictures and words that appeal to you. Look for things that inspire you and places you want to visit. There is no right or wrong choice; all these things are going to resonate with you. It is important to mention that you should be focusing on how you want to feel, not just the things that you want. Maybe you want to feel more confident or more thankful, filled with gratitude in your daily living. Maybe you want to go back to school, or finish your degree, or start your own business.

Once you have gathered your collage of images that appeal to you, you will need a bulletin board, a poster board, or several pieces of paper as well as scissors and glue or tape to start making your creative visualization. Write down whatever you are wanting in order to know exactly what to include on your board. Meditate and daydream about all the things you want to be, do, or have. Imagine your ideal career, relationship, house, car, community, body, et cetera. The more specific you can be, the better!

You want to be in a good headspace when you sit down to make your vision board. After you create your vision board, spend a few minutes reviewing what you have placed on the board; maybe you want to take something off. This will aid you in visualizing your goals and seeing them as achieved in your mind's-eye.

Place your completed board where you can see it often to be reminded of your vision and goals. This will now become your source of motivation to keep working toward and ultimately accomplishing them, trusting that the Universe will provide you with the opportunities to manifest each and every thing you truly desire. I have found my vision board very helpful when I lose sight of my dreams. It has been a great inspiration for me when I forget how good things can be in life if I just hang in there.

I have my moments of low motivation also, and nothing is wrong with that. Sometimes, our body is trying to tell us to slow down and balance out a little. The power of a vision permits us to see beyond our present condition. Through visioning, we can dream, create, and manifest what does not yet exist. However, the vision must hold steady to the true and the good. If we want positive results, we must hold true to positive outcomes. The vision must be powerful enough to create a conviction so strong within that it cannot be shattered regardless of appearances.

Stay focused.

I am and I will. I shall be exactly as happy as I decide to be.

Visualize who you want to be;
then work for it! Hold on to
your vision; this life is your
one chance to make it happen.
Don't let fear, doubt, or a few
setbacks prevent you from
reaching your goals.
You can do this!

PERSEVERANCE, RESILIENCE & COURAGE WITH GRACE

Reflections

Was this chapter insightful or inspiring?

Your thoughts:

CHAPTER

4

Goals and Planning

One day as he sat counting,
he heard a noise.
"Shhh!" he said. "I'm counting!"
The noise went on and on.
Ant opened the door,
and there on his lawn stood
a grasshopper, playing a fiddle.
"Well, I never," said Ant.
GOALS

PLANS
"Well, I always," said Grasshopper.
"It's June, Ant! The sun is warm; the sky is blue,
Come out and dance----I'll play for you!"
"Humph!" said Ant. "You should be storing up
food for the winter, not fiddling around, wasting
time."

Human success depends on having lifetime goals and making the necessary changes to accomplish them over a given period of time. A *goal* is a time-bound, anticipated, desired result one sets and works toward achieving.

The preceding image illustrates an industrious ant with a goal and plan for the future. The ant stores enough food for the winter, while the grasshopper lives his life with neither plans nor goals, dancing and having a good time with no thought for the winter months.

The process of setting goals helps you choose where you want to go in life by knowing precisely what you want to achieve and where you have to concentrate your efforts. Setting a goal implies that you desire change, but remember that each goal should have a purpose. Align your plan to fit your goals. Take some time, at least once a month, to ensure that your goals are still pointing you in the direction of your priorities and life purpose. If they are not, review and alter your vision and your plans.

Setting goals gives you the possibility of bringing your dreams and prospects to life. It creates motivation and provides you with certainty that the final outcome will be worthwhile. Goals must be structured so that you can realistically reach them within the expected time, allowing for evaluation for change of plans.

In my experience, the tried-and-proven elements of goal planning are personal on all levels. Goals may be short term or long term, which eventually satisfies your lifetime plans.

My negative experience of 2018–2020 did not permit me to evaluate or modify my goals at the time. It catapulted me from the height of my greatest achievement of independence to what I considered an abysmal position. I was in unfamiliar territory. I realized that I was at the crossroads of my life. My thoughts were raging daily, until William Ernest Henley's poem "Invictus" reminded me that through extraordinarily challenging circumstances, "I am the master of my faith, / I am the captain of my soul." It was then that I decided I could not move forward until I developed the courage to let go of the negative past and start all over again—and PRC was born, and my pain became my purpose!

I then vowed that my present situation would not be my final destination. With my vast cache of knowledge and experiences, and my new vision, I decided to develop a plan—setting new goals to produce successful outcomes, as outlined in this motivational manifesto, hoping to impart how I overcame the most difficult experiences of my life.

We all want to live more successful, happier, and more confident lives, so we ask, "How can my personal life goals help me do this?" Whatever goals you choose, depend on the area of your life you most want to focus on right now. It is important to remember that your goals will most likely shift and change as your priorities do; that's OK. The following are a few topic areas about which you may set personal goals.

- Family and lifestyle
- Health and fitness
- Relationship and spirituality
- Career or business

Have a vision, write it down with an expected date, and break it down into steps; this now becomes our plan of action to make your dreams come true. Visualize your goals on a daily basis as if you have already achieved them; then align your purpose and values with your plan of action. This is where vision boards are helpful. You can even tape onto it cutouts of images that you admire and aspire tobecome. Use them as inspirations.

Keep yourself accountable by sharing your dreams, goals, and plan with someone you can trust who wishes you well and wants to see you succeed. Seek out a mentor or life coach who will support and encourage you through frustrations or roadblocks. The right support team can help you transform obstacles into opportunities while keeping you on track. The goal-setting process helps you choose where you want to go in life. By knowing exactly what you want to achieve, you know in what areas you have to concentrate your efforts. You will also quickly spot the distractions that can so easily lead you astray.

Track your progress by having a set schedule to review both short- and long-term goals. This will help you determine what activities are helping or hindering. It is important to know when you need to recalibrate your path. Stay committed to your goals and plans. Do not lose sight of your ultimate goal; remember life is happening for you, not to you!

Celebrate your successes when you have achieved each goal. That will help you stay focused while being present in the moment. Goal setting is important as you get older. It allows for reflecting on time not used constructively and on regrets of not achieving the things you were capable of having. Setting goals helps trigger new behaviors and guides your focus while sustaining momentum in life.

Remember that failing to meet a goal is not a failure in life, per se, just as long as you learn from that experience and apply the lessons learned to the process of your new set of goals. Bear in mind that goals can change as time goes on. Adjust them regularly to reflect growth in your knowledge and experience, and if a goal does not hold any interest for you any longer, consider letting it go.

Success comes when you learn from your failures. Through hard work, struggles, and sacrifices with good goal planning, you can achieve. Even if you have setbacks (like I experienced), you will be able to regain your position because you know it's worth it. When confronted with failures, think of what's next rather than brooding over your failures.

Consider your goals a vehicle to success.

You must have a specific plan to achieve your goals. Set realistic goals that are attainable to grow into the person you aspire to be. The pursuit of a goal enables you to become something better; put your future into your own hands! Become the person you most want to be as you arrive at your desired destination.

PERSEVERANCE, RESILIENCE & COURAGE WITH GRACE

Reflections

Was this chapter insightful or inspiring?

Your thoughts:

CHAPTER

5

Purpose

Life is like a Butterfly.
You go through changes before
you become something beautiful.

"The Lord will fulfill his
purpose for me" PSALM 138:8

You have to be a caterpillar before you can become a butterfly. It would be great to walk right into our purpose at birth, but unfortunately, or to our great fortune, we need to evolve through many processes to arrive at our destined purpose.

The foundation for the butterfly is the caterpillar, a squirmy, single-minded, hungry worm. Its purpose: to become as large as possible to fuel the beautiful creature that will emerge. Metamorphosis, the change we all go through to become different, is our growth! The inspirational image of the caterpillar that turns into the butterfly can be likened to our life's evolving processes in order to fulfill our intended purpose.

As we take our first breath, we enter into existence, which expires at the last breath. What we plan and execute with passion or a lack thereof between the first and last breaths is our life's *purpose*, which is unique for everyone. This time is important to our contribution on earth, and ultimately our family.

We may face seemingly insurmountable challenges, but we must persevere through them all. Understanding our purpose, we must forge on, face the challenges, to reach new horizons. Our purpose can actually shift and change throughout life in response to the evolving priorities of our experiences. Purpose and destiny are linked.

Each living person has a different purpose in life. We all have heard the saying, "You were born for such a time as this." Nonetheless, it has been my experience and understanding that purpose is the central motivating aim of our lives. Purpose shapes our goals, offers a sense of direction, and influences our behavior.

After my traumatic experiences of recent years, I struggled with repeated, agonizing questions, such as, "What is my purpose now?" The trials and tribulations that visited me made me question my existence on life's journey. I started cultivating mindfulness. I acquired this by training my mind to focus its attention on the present moment while accepting the reality of my situation. Being mindful helped me fully engage in positive activities that gave me a greater capacity to deal with the adverse experiences.

I became less likely to be occupied with negativity about my future and regrets over the past, realizing or learning that, in each person's life, there are things that give us pause and make us take note. My misfortune or opportunity propelled me on this new life's journey to awaken in finding my new purpose. I found out that it is never too late to live my best life while working through the process. Finding my purpose became an exciting journey rather than a stressful goal. I ceased existing as the victim, realizing that some circumstances in my life result from my own decisions, not anyone else's. Fulfillment followed when I took responsibility for seeking my purpose instead of focusing on the psychological and spiritual assault I encountered. I kept reminding myself of Genesis 50:20: "You meant evil against me; but God used it for good, in order to bring about, as it is this day." I was once unable to see beyond the adversities, but now, I can see and understand clearly my *purpose* and *destiny*!

The caterpillar understands only what it is experiencing. It has no concept of the great beyond. Getting enough leaves to eat each day is all that occupies its mind. Survival is its purpose. The caterpillar does not have an easy life, and just when it is getting comfortable with that life, change happens! It does not understand why or how but goes along with the process. The process may be frighteningly different; there may be something scary about this new environmental change. The caterpillar may wonder, *What is happening to me? Is this all there is to life? Is this the end?*

Part of finding your purpose is accepting your limitations. Get to know yourself, taking the role of observer. As you practice self-compassion while building self-awareness, you shall be able to find the meaning you are seeking. *Self-compassion* means being patient and gentle with yourself. Everyone who has ever asked themselves, "What is my purpose?" began from a place of uncertainty. Their hesitancy is what prompted them to dig deep and find greater meaning.

It is at that moment the caterpillar's intended purpose is revealed. Emerging from the darkness of its ordeal, feeling the newness of itself, and understanding the possibilities of its new body, it achieves the purpose. A beautiful butterfly emerges!

The process of metamorphosis teaches us that if we want to reach any goal, we need to patiently work through the process. We must have the hunger for knowledge, just like the caterpillar had for leaves. Shedding the old and welcoming the new is essential, and most importantly, we must have patience when we are tested. All that is to say a caterpillar may not look the same as a butterfly, but it's a work in progress. A caterpillar grows into a butterfly, albeit at a much faster rate than we transform. We need to work for it and also be patient.

Basically, at some point, every butterfly was a caterpillar. While the image of literal mammalian metamorphosis might be silly, a philosophical interpretation is not. The human concept of redemption—the idea that we can change for the better—can be read into the caterpillar-to-butterfly progression.

Whether you are considering your life's purpose for the first time or wanting to expand on your current purpose, this motivational manifesto is filled with treasures of understanding the human journey and brings forth a broad spectrum of tools for self-discovery. Whether you are a young adult just starting out in life or you are approaching midlife, you can garner something positive from this motivational manifesto. This is a little bit about divine purpose and a good exercise in understanding your true self and your unique life's purpose.

We are all created by the hand of God on purpose; we are each an unrepeatable miracle. Let us infuse our life with good purpose!

They Wanted Her To

Change Back Into What

She Had Always Been....

A Caterpillar; But The

Caterpillar Thought Not

Of The Process,

She Had To Go Through,

To Become A Beautiful Butterfly.

She Had Achieved Her Purpose!!

PERSEVERANCE, RESILIENCE & COURAGE WITH GRACE

Reflections

Was this chapter insightful or inspiring?

Your thoughts:

6

Changing Your Perspective

EMBRACE CHANGE

*"God Promises to make something good out of the storms that bring devastation to your life."
~Romans 8:28*

I love you
to pieces!

While reading this motivational manifesto, have you made any impactful life changes that have left you happier and more resilient? Nothing changes if you change nothing!

Do not be deterred if you have not. There are many bumps on the road to becoming your best self. Just be intentional about learning from them through PRC. You should be thinking and setting goals differently while tapping into your inner strength with resilience and determination. Recalibrate your path!

Acknowledge that every person has their own perspective and opinions that are formed based on their experiences. My advice is to know that you have the power to form your own perspective, as this knowledge can be very freeing and may provide you a great deal of comfort to go forward in life. For example, if you have the tendency to be negative, you can actively take steps to see the positive and let go of negativity, thereby changing your perspective into a positive one.

Without knowledge, you cannot grow or develop, and educating yourself broadly will help you most effectively reformulate your perspective. The key to shifting your perspective is to remember what your goal is—what you are aimimg for. For example, a job where you perform mundane tasks will continue being mundane if you see it as "just a job." But with the right attitude or thinking, you could regard it as a way to learn skills you may need in the future; then it is no longer just a job. It is an opportunity to learn. Nothing physical changed, just your perspective—and that makes all the difference.

I believe that our paths have crossed because you may benefit from some of this information. The purpose of this motivational manifesto is to give you the nudge … a push that gets you moving in the direction of your dreams. Our lives are reflections of our thoughts. Changing our thinking changes our lives. Within us lies the power to make positive changes in our lives that will lead us to our purpose. In chapter 1, I did say that you are your best advocate;

develop the muscle of encouraging yourself to be better and do better with your life.

We are living in unprecedented times. The years 2020–2022 have been very challenging for all of us. No one could have predicted a worldwide pandemic with such a catastrophic impact. This pandemic has changed the way we live. It has brought many things into proper perspective and has shown many of us what is most important in life. During quarantine and social distancing, I have had lots of time to reflect on the past, work on the present, and plan for a new future. I am determined to make the necessary changes to live a better life now and after the pandemic.

There is no greater time than now to start moving toward our best life. Let us stop waiting for tomorrow, because it is not guaranteed. Stop waiting for someone to give you permission; they may never show up. Stop waiting for the perfect moment; it may never come.

Every choice you make through Perseverance, Resilience, and Courage going forward will make a difference in your life. While working on becoming your best self, you have to change the way you look at things. Think positively, with gratitude. Always be thankful. You were uniquely designed for success when you were created for this purpose of life's choosing. Align your life with your God-given gifts, which will empower you to achieve anything you set your heart on accomplishing. Keep remembering that our thinking process creates the world we have. We cannot change that world for good or bad without changing our thinking.

We greatly reduce our power to change and progress if we harvest a victim mindset. We must eradicate the victim mindset, which dilutes human potential. We must take personal responsibility for all circumstances, good or bad.

God has our past covered and our future secured. We do not have to be afraid anymore. As the scripture teaches us, "If God is for you, who can be against you?" (Romans 8:31).

A simple change in how we look at events and occurrences can greatly enhance our lives. It is all about *perspective*, what we choose to focus on. It has been said that perspective is 10 percent what happens to us in life and 90 percent how we choose to perceive the experience or respond to it. This is not always easy, but it is a process that is worth the time and effort needed for a positive outcome.

All human beings are confronted with negative thoughts every once in a while. Unfortunately, because of the changing times that we are now living in, negative thinking seems to be increasing, which can yield a destructive thought pattern. This can decrease our confidence, thereby affecting our mood and general outlook on life. By means of constant negative thinking, we can become less confident, and our behavior in the outside world can start to reflect our inner thoughts.

Thankfully, we can use the very same principles to our advantage. We can do exactly the opposite of what we think with the aid of positive affirmations. Therefore, instead of entertaining negative thoughts that will drag you down, use the power of positive affirmations that will surely affect profoundly favorable changes in your life. Positive affirmations rewire our brains. They allow us to restructure the very thinking processes that greatly influence our behaviors. Positive affirmations motivate us, inspire us, and encourage us to take action, make changes, and help us realize our goals.

I strongly believe that what you think, you become. Words and thoughts have power. So instead of talking yourself into believing that you are unworthy, introduce positive thoughts, and before long, you will recognize great benefits in becoming your best self. Create your own affirmations. All it takes is to identify an area of your life with which you are not satisfied. Create a list of all the negative qualities that you wish to change. Include justified criticisms. Keep in mind that affirmations are meant to help you overcome negative thinking. For this reason, they should be positive, specific, relevant, short, and achievable.

I believe in and recommend creating vision boards and personal mission statements. Here are some suggestions for other positive behaviors.

- Spend quiet time with yourself, preferably outside. Relax and absorb the beauty of the natural world (the trees, birds, et cetera).
- Start by looking within. Think about your values and beliefs, and come up with questions and answers for yourself, such as the whys, whats, and hows.
- Envision the wonderful life you want to live with yourself and family while becoming your best self. Make the relevant changes.
- Remind yourself that the unexamined life is just surviving, not thriving. To unlock your full potential and achieve your greatest dreams, you need to take a step back and examine the kind of life you are now living.

- Choose the life you desire in order to experience your best self, and work toward it.
- Set your goals, and plan how you are going to achieve these exciting thoughts.
- Identify your interests and strengths, and work toward them step by step.

People do the best they can with what they know. Once you have decided on your path and fully committed, frequently inventory your progress. Focus on what is working and what isn't. Do not be disappointed when some of your plans are not working according to your expectations. *Embrace change.* Keep going until it works out for you in the end. Remain flexible along the way. The path you take is never a straight line—learning from mistakes, embracing failure, and using negativity as a driving force for change, recalibrate your path. As long as you are making progress, you are going in the right direction.

True power comes from within, and reprogramming your brain conditions you for success. Sometimes, frustration becomes a gift, teaching us patience. Failure becomes a lesson, counseling us on how to be better in the future. Some roadblocks are opportunities for us to pivot and find new creative solutions. That is the power of our mind's dedication to resolve.

Every day, we face situations that require a decision, whether it be regarding school, work, family, money, or relationships, which can create stress. Changing our negative perspective toward these things can make all the difference. Perception is reality. The manner in which we view some things becomes the truth in our lives; this sometimes can be become self-limiting. When you change your view of the world, you change how you feel about it.

Major life changes shake up our world. They did mine, as is evident in my life experiences. Such changes invite or pressure us to interact with life in new ways, resulting in growth.

Before I underwent my major psychological change, I thought that I could control the outcome of every situation. Now, when I experience major failures in life, I prayerfully go through the process with faith, believing and knowing there is a lesson to be learned, which will make me stronger, wiser, and more resilient. I choose gratitude and appreciation over criticism and fear. I am a work in progress; being aware of all my blessings and embracing change give me the opportunity to move in a more fulfilling direction toward creating my better self. In this way, PRC was born.

From my pain, I have found my purpose to live my best life as I become my best self. Remember that opinions don't change the world, but actions do, as you become the change you seek. All it takes to start a tidal wave of change in your life is a small, simple shift in perception. You will begin to rewire your mind, transform your thinking, and reconnect with your soul. You can make the shift from seeing what is wrong about something to seeing what is right. You can shift from focusing on what you don't have to focusing on what you have. You can shift from the energy of fear to a space of love. The minute you change your focus and energy, the whole world around you also shifts to reflect that—*perspective*!

A change in perspective isn't quite as simple as turning yourself upside down, but removing yourself from a situation and looking at it differently can be your best strategy toward gaining control. Once you give yourself some perspective, you can take steps to make necessary changes or decide to accept the things you cannot change. Daily gratitude is a powerful exercise that will help you keep your perspective in line. Giving yourself a new perspective can open up new possibilities as well as generate ideas you haven't thought of as yet. It can help you improve a relationship with someone, calm you down when you are stressed, and even help you enjoy and appreciate all the good things you already have.

It makes me think, in an odd sort of way, how perspective is everything. You have the power to change the way you think to benefit the good you seek. *Be transformed or changed by the renewing of your mind* (Romans 12:2).

It all starts with you; decide what you want to do, and make this gift of life count. The mind is everything. What you think, you will become!

Change your perspective on some of your challenges, and you will see your circumstances change. You cannot live a positive life with a negative mindset. You have the power to change your story. The world is a reflection of your thinking ... you choose!

PERSEVERANCE, RESILIENCE & COURAGE WITH GRACE

Reflections

Was this chapter insightful or inspiring?

Your thoughts:

CHAPTER
7
Seasons of Your Life

To Everything There Is A
Season
A Time For Every Purpose Under
Heaven
Ecclesiastes 3:1
He has made
Everything Beautiful
In Its Time...
Ecclesiastes 3:11

We are always experiencing a season in our lives. It matters not what season we are in; no season lasts forever. Change is on its way.

Seasons are times when new opportunities that may be beneficial to your life's journey arise. By becoming aware of them, learning from them, and applying what we learn from them, we can no doubt achieve a very fulfilling life. We must resolve to live, not just endure, each season of our lives.

Through the seasons of my life's experiences, I have grown to realize that my seasons of adversity were really where my pain became my purpose. I have learned things in my dark seasons that have enabled me to minister hope and stability to others who have faced similar uncomfortable experiences. So, do not despair if you have trials. There are always lessons to be learned. Know that God is with you in these times and will bring you through.

Life is unpredictable. It changes with the seasons. Sometimes, even your worst experience happens for the best of reasons (even if you don't understand that then). Although at the time it feels like you will not survive, be reminded that tough moments don't define you. Trust yourself; you are stronger than you think. Keep reminding yourself of the parts of your journey that pushed you to overcome difficulties in the past. That is what I did!

In challenging times, when everything appears to be working against us (such as our health, money, friends, and family), we wonder, *What is going on?* It is during those trying seasons that our character often grows the most. From the pain, we may discover our purpose and understand God's plans for ordaining the seasons. As it is written in Ecclesiastes 3:1, "To everything there is a Season, a time for every Purpose under the sun."

During the seasons of our lives, we are more likely to engage in some reflection, which will help us determine what we want to achieve in the coming years or the next season. It is through these experiences that we develop self-confidence as we grow, which is necessary for us to live comfortably in our own skin and not worry about what other people think.

We must seek to understand the seasons of our life. Understanding that everyone experiences change and transition in life, helps us not to draw the wrong conclusions about what is happening, during our seasons or the reasons for it.

Sometimes, life is exciting and dynamic, and we feel on top of the world. At other times, we just want to withdraw and escape the situation; but never let the season you are experiencing define who you are. Learn from every season. Every season has lessons of life for us.

An example of seasons in the book of Genesis depicts a young man whose name was Joseph. God's plan was that Joseph would be a ruler. However, the record shows that he underwent a series of traumatic seasons before he could experience God's ultimate plan. His season of prosperity was achieved after his adverse experiences of the pits and prison. God's plans don't change because *seasons* do!

Do not change what you believe according to the season you are in. We do not control everything in life. There are lots of things we can't control. That is life, but we must always remember PRC: Perseverance, Resilience, and Courage! Sometimes, bad decisions are made in tough seasons. When you are in a challenging or difficult season, be careful what meaning you give to things in the tough seasons of God!

Most of the time, our experiences in our seasons are meant to be only part of our life's journey, which can be a chapter in our story. Do not be impatient during your seasons. Expand your faith while preparing for the best outcome. Each season of life teaches us lessons about ourselves, other people, and life in general. It helps us transform psychologically, physically, and socially. It strengthens our souls and resilience and enlivens our spirits in the face of adversity.

We celebrate when we succeed and we complain when we fail, but eventually, we start to really consider who we are, what we want out of life, and how we want to move forward. The seasons of life shape our character and lay the framework for the good life we envision ahead of us. Most importantly, they help us evolve successfully.

From birth to our midtwenties, we are in the spring of our lives. This is where we are nourished by education and formative experiences. This is our season of learning and growing, a time to focus on ourselves and discover who we are and what we want out of life as people. This is an acceptable time to be selfish and make mistakes from which we can learn and move on. This season serves to shape our character and lay the foundation for the life we are hoping to experience - Evolution.

Engage in proper planning and preparation for the future. Make sure you are making well-thought-out decisions or choices; this is not the time to be impulsive. Do a sufficient amount of self-reflection, which will help you correct your path if there are any missteps … Recalibrate!

Here are some actions to take to get the most out of your seasons of life.

- Be intentional about everything you do to set the stage for a healthy life.
- Be mindful of the people with whom you associate, the places you go, and the things you do.
- Take advantage of everything available to you that is positive.
- Most importantly, take care of your body, soul, and mind.

Life is full of contrasts. We go through mountains and valleys, successes and failures, wins and losses. In the weather, there are four seasons, but in our lives, there are lots of different seasons that include both good and bad times. God can take the bad things and turn them around, using them for the good intended.

What truly matters is your mindset. As long as you don't look at yourself as too young or too old, then you're not. I believe that each season has its own strengths and weaknesses. You just need to leverage your strengths and learn to cope with your weaknesses.

The seasons of life are about the transitions you go through and how they impact your mindset and actions. The amount of time it takes to move through each season is a reflection of your state of mind. Furthermore, the seasons are about the process of transition from one set of circumstances to the next, allowing for opportunities to learn, evolve, and eventually reap the rewards of a well-lived life.

Ultimately, life is about transformation. Every experience, despite its magnitude, helps us grow on many levels, which paves the way for richer experiences that will challenge us to overcome the obstacles that life inevitably sends our way.

No matter who you are and what season you are in, believe that you can achieve the success you want. Now, don't just think about your season; embrace it, and let it work for you. Allow yourself to feel satisfied with your life as you acknowledge the wisdom you have obtained. Take action today!

Be transformed through the seasons of your life!

We cannot change the circumstances, seasons, or the wind, but we can change ourselves. Just like the seasons, people have the ability to change. Embrace the season you are experiencing, and let go when it is over. Embrace the opportunity to begin again. Life is to be lived and celebrated. All seasons are beautiful, giving us the opportunity to appreciate change, shedding our old ways, and become renewed. Life is short, time is fast, no replay, no rewind ... so enjoy every moment of your season!

PERSEVERANCE, RESILIENCE & COURAGE WITH GRACE

Reflections

Was this chapter insightful or inspiring?

Your thoughts:

8

Maintaining Your Successful Momentum

Your success is measured by the strength of your desire; the size of your dream; and how you handle disappointment along the way.

I have chosen to use the horse to speak to perceived changes in the race of life. The horse, including its momentum, symbolizes power, grace, beauty, nobility, strength, and freedom. If your reading of

PRC has influenced no major changes, but some small adjustments, that is OK; you are on a successful path, which you should maintain. It is my hope that this motivational manifesto will help move you along to becoming the very best version of yourself.

The little boy shown in the preceding image is an example of the goodness of God's promises. He is my new grandson, with whom God has truly blessed me, after losing my first grandson ten years ago. He exhibits freedom of love, a resilient spirit, and some of the horse's attributes.

A horse maintains its strides, and even when slowing down, it does so with dignity. The horse presents nobility without conceit, friendship without envy, and beauty without vanity. Having a spirit of freedom with limitless energy, the horse is a resilient force. Horses like to live in herds, reminding us that we should not alienate others by being alone. Strong, powerful, and beautiful, the horse has the capability to give us an escape from our mundane existence.

Now that you have become the architect of your own life with Perseverance, Resilience, and Courage; established your vision; planned your goals with purpose; and made any necessary changes, we shall discuss maintaining your successful momentum. You should measure your success by the strength of your desire, the size of your dream, and the manner in which you handle disappointment.

People who succeed have momentum with direction. The more they succeed, the more they want to succeed. Success is all about having momentum and understanding the key to maintaining it. The cycle of success shows that what you do impacts your choices ...

and your results. In other words, you reap what you sow. This applies to life in general. There is no success without the passion to be successful, and when you realize that you have achieved your goals, you must maintain. That's how you build momentum.

Create your momentum, and then focus on maintaining it by doing the following.

- Nurture your sense of fulfillment with pride and excellence.
- Compete only with yourself, seeking to improve your personal standards.
- Accept compliments, but do not depend on others' approval for validation.
- Establish a reliable team that understands the nature of and requirements for maintaining your established standards. Your team must also be interested in your success and happy to be associated with it.
- Network with people of similar ambitions and interests.
- Be vigilant.
- Be quick to notice deviation from the required standards or norms.
- Repeat the steps that brought you to the realization of success.

Successful people strive to maintain a positive focus in life regardless of what is going on around them. They focus on past successes instead of past failures. They never encourage the thinking that they have arrived at their goal and now nothing else matters.

The continuous stream of individual choices people make from day to day determines the outcome of their experiences. Successful people always keep their goals in perspective and align their thinking and purpose. They may need to revise their goals from time to time, and that is OK. They are specific in their goal setting, and they have a clear vision of their results. They are willing to adjust their schedule if it is in conflict.

Whatever goal and process end up bringing you to your destination, review and balance are required to maintain what you have worked very hard to achieve. From time to time, you need to refer back to the ideas and resources that brought you to this level of success.

Write down your definition of *success*. What does succeeding mean to you? Success means different things to different people. For example, my definition of success is bringing a vision to reality. Since it is my vision, I don't let other people impose their ideas on my desired results. In so doing, I can successfully build on my earlier achievements and continually improve my performance and results.

I have met some people who believe that success is cyclical and that for every up, there must be a down; therefore, trying to improve our performance and results in a sustainable way is foolish and idealistic. I ask, *Why can't we set a goal to continually improve our results and continuously maintain positive momentum?* We should not lose sight of the very process or path that helped us achieve our goals; we should maintain the process that brought us to a successful threshold.

With a little care, all that extra effort won't become an everyday expectation. If you are willing to prioritize other parts of your life, then you can build on your successes and keep some momentum without overworking yourself. I encourage you to always take responsibility for your results, regardless of whether they are good or bad. This allows you to see what adjustments you need to make in order to steadily improve toward the desired results.

You must have a clear and compelling purpose for anything you want and are doing in any aspect of your life; if not, you will lose interest in maintaining the energy necessary to continually improve.

Your vision, goals, plans, and purpose make up a large part of your engine for generating sustainable success. Be aware of what you are good at doing and what you are passionate about. Then spend as much time and energy as you can using your strengths and passions to fulfill your purpose and drive better results.

Don't think of achieving sustainable success as some pie-in-the-sky wish; instead, think of it as a process that you must carefully watch over and execute with discipline and balance. As you do that, you will steadily get better at maintaining it. In time, you will be able to increase the momentum of realizing your desired outcomes without falling backward. The more success you have in any area of your life, the more likely you are to exude confidence. Therein lies your momentum to maintain that level.

Remember your mindset is all you need to fuel an ongoing upward trajectory. This supports Newton's law of movement: "An object in motion stays in motion; an object at rest stays at rest." Be aware of your mental health. It is easier to maintain momentum than to rebuild it once lost. Mindfulness changes the emotional lives of our brains.

Here are a few suggestions regarding protecting your mental health.

- Meditate and pray daily. Start your day with gratitude for being.
- Think positively. Surround yourself with positive people.
- Talk about what is bothering you. Do not be afraid to ask for or seek help.
- Remain resilient. Learn from your mistakes. Identify your triggers.
- Do not complicate your life unnecessarily. Laugh often.
- Exercise daily. It enhances your mental and physical well-being.
- Set realistic goals for yourself, and pursue your dreams.
- Get adequate rest or sleep, and eat healthy.
- Do not give up!

Good luck!

Develop and maintain momentum by working continuously toward your desired goals. It is easier to maintain momentum than rebuild it once it is lost. In order to achieve our objectives, we must keep the momentum going. Successful people know that momentum is necessary to succeed. A loss of momentum is often a loss of perspective. Dreams don't work unless you do ... get the momentum going! Consistency is the key to achieving and maintaining momentum.

PERSEVERANCE, RESILIENCE & COURAGE WITH GRACE

Reflections

Was this chapter insightful or inspiring?

Your thoughts:

CHAPTER
9

PRC Inspired—The Courageous and Resilient Woman

Perseverance Resilience And Courage With Grace

"In Memory Of My Mother, The First Courageous & Resilient Woman I Have Known"

In this chapter, I pay tribute to the most courageous and resilient woman I have known, my mother, Lilian. She single-handedly raised twelve children, after she became a single parent, with the help of God. My mother soldiered on, even when times were tough. She demonstrated a positive demeanor, always pleasant, sharing funny childhood memories to make everyone laugh. No one knew the challenges she endured as a single parent, the hurt and pain she hid from her children, remaining courageous and resilient. Whether by choice or by happenstance, my mother was a village all by herself, of course with the support of my grandparents, my uncles, and constant prayers.

She believed she could, and she did! Defined by no one else, she is her own story, blazing through the world, turning history into her-story, your story. And when people dare to tell her all the things she cannot be, she will smile and courageously tell them, "I am a PRC woman; you cannot stop me." In this way, you will become the heroine of your own story. Keep going, more determined than before. You cannot go back and change the beginning, but you can surely start where you are now and change the ending.

Living takes courage. There are times when trials and tribulations test us on our life's journey; I have been tested! Maybe you have lost your job, your business has failed, or your family life has involved discord or a divorce, and the last thing you feel like doing is mustering the courage to go on. But luckily, you do not have to look far; the courage lies within you *Courage* is a necessity to overcome fear and achieve a desired goal, but it does not mean recklessly taking risks without sensible precautions. Positive courage helps us achieve our expected goals, being brave in the face of fear.

Resilience is the quality to remain strong in a situation that knocks you down in life. Resilient people recover more easily from tough moments and stand stronger than before, rather than resigning to failure or self-pity. They use those challenges to explore other courses for navigating their endeavors to succeed. They recalibrate their path. Some characteristics of resilient people include having self-esteem, embracing change, being optimistic, and considering failure as one of life's teachers. Self-esteem and positive belief in your abilities can help you cope with stress and recover from a difficult experience faster.

Generally, women are known to be courageous; we have always been fearless, understanding nothing is more resilient than the human spirit. We are not what happened to us; we are what we choose to become. We were put on this earth to achieve our greatest self, to live out our purpose, and to do it fearlessly.

The importance of courage coupled with fearlessness is written and stressed in the Bible. Examples are Deuteronomy 31:16 ("Be strong and be of good courage, fear not") and Joshua 1:19 ("Have not I commanded thee? Be strong and of good courage; be not afraid [fearless], neither be thou dismayed").

Also, courage is depicted by women in the Bible. For example, Abigail was courageous and wise; Esther was brave. Deborah's courage is legendary. These women inspired others and also demonstrated how to live with rock-solid faith, even in the toughest of circumstances. They experienced fear at some points, but they knew it is part of being human. No matter how overwhelmed that fear may have made them feel, they were able to break through and become change agents.

These women may have lived in a completely different society and time than we do, but we can learn a great deal from their stories. We see through their stories that we may not live a life that is absent of fear, but we can trust God and not allow fear to stop us from achieving great things while living our best life courageously.

We should never undervalue each other. Courage comes from God. We are encouraged to be courageous, fearless, and resilient, just like those women, when we face whatever life throws at us, seeking grace with confidence so we may receive mercy to help us in our times of need.

We courageous women are open-minded and not afraid of considering alternatives; we embrace new perspectives and are secure knowing that we have the ability and freedom to choose a new direction, if necessary. Our courage comes from knowing that we can handle whatever we encounter because we were designed by our creator not only to handle pain but also to be resilient.

Being a courageous woman means being resilient and fearless in the face of adversity, pain, and struggle; handling any challenge with grace and poise; and turning to others for support when needed. By embodying these principles, we all can become PRC inspired. A courageous woman knows that perseverance and resilience are needed prescriptions for success. She will keep an eye toward the big picture while being patient and persistent.

A woman who possesses courage and resilience, while being fearless, is a woman of substance. Do not define her by the way she looks; she is more than what meets the eye. Define her by the tough battles she faces each day and her courage to face and overcome them, no matter how difficult. She will survive.

She is not perfect but complete. She realizes everything she needs to fulfill her life's mission can be found within. She has uncovered her powers and knows how to use them. She is no longer on the path but has become the path. The PRC-inspired woman is stronger than the temptations she faces and greater than the distractions coming against whatever she is trying to accomplish. She has what it takes to stay focused, finish, and *win*!

The PRC-inspired woman lives one of Maya Angelou's poems as her daily inspiration, "And Still I Rise": "You may shoot me with your words, / You may cut me with your eyes, / You may kill me with your hatefulness, / But still, like air, I'll rise."

You are a woman of strength, courage, and dignity ... very resilient! You value yourself and fight for what you believe in. You will never give up on your dreams, regardless of how many obstacles stand in your way. Adversity and suffering are two of life's greatest teachers; they teach us how to become resilient, to grow better, not bitter, learning how to strive, survive, and overcome the unexpected. A courageous and resilient woman knows that the first step of getting what she wants is having the courage to get rid of what she doesn't. The courage of a woman is inspiring ... she possesses the determination of not giving up.

PERSEVERANCE, RESILIENCE & COURAGE WITH GRACE

Reflections

Was this chapter insightful or inspiring?

Your thoughts:

10

Becoming Your Best Self— Recalibrate Your Path

"I Can, I Will And I Have!!" "I Believed I Could And I Did!!"

"I am not what happened to me; I am what I choose to become."

Now that you have followed the PRC prescription, it is my hope that you feel encouraged and are on your path to creating your best self.

The preceding image captures the exhilaration of results when Perseverance, Resilience, and Courage are your constant companions. Continue to be the architect of the best life you envision, applauding the outcome as you successfully follow the path of PRC's prescription.

Our ultimate goal in life should be to become our best self. Our immediate goal should be to get on the path that will lead us there. Becoming our best self is a lifelong journey. It doesn't have a particular start or end; but since we are discussing this journey, I suggest that you start now, if you are not already on this path.

Working on ourselves is a continuous process, and indeed cannot happen overnight. While writing this chapter, I totally admit that I, too, am a work in progress and continue to be on the journey of becoming my best self. However, on this journey of self-discovery, I have often found myself recalibrating my path. I have learned so much more than I initially expected as I have worked through the process. Today, I am proud of the woman I am becoming because I have gone through one hell of a time becoming her!

What does it mean to be your best self and live your best life? In my mind, being your best self is coming as close as you can to fulfilling your innate potential while maximizing the possibilities for happiness and success in all areas of your life, including spirituality and wellness.

As far as your "best self" goes, there is no one-size-fits-all definition. Instead, the description is entirely personal. Your best self will never be the same as someone else's. Keep in mind that we are all different. We possess different skills and talents. Each of us encounters different challenges as we go along life's journey. Therefore, when defining your best self, be reminded that you get to choose what that means for you. Better still, your definition doesn't need to be fixed in stone. Instead, it will almost certainly change over time. As you achieve goals, check your list, and revise your goals or ideals. You will uncover more and more about who you really are, resulting in your best-self definition.

I started practicing self-improvement when I realized I needed to take my time to figure out my journey toward becoming my best self. Doing that took much pressure of performance off my shoulders. I took baby steps, giving myself permission to work at my own pace. I continuously referred to PRC.

- **Perseverance:** Not giving up; investing time and effort in myself
- **Resilience:** Having the ability to bounce back from adversity; learning from my past mistakes; turning lemons into lemonade
- **Courage:** Acting on self-discipline; paying attention to my mental, physical, emotional, and spiritual well-being

In addition, I was inspired by listening to great motivational speakers, reading their books, admiring their lives, and emulating their good habits. It was only when I started on my path to self-discovery that I realized the journey does not come with a handy manual. Mine depended on the inner work that I was willing to do. And yes, that's the tough work, coming face-to-face with the rhetoric that you believe and the harsh reality of things that you have to unlearn, but this is absolutely necessary on the journey to becoming your best self. Change your mindset; know your values.

I learned that being your best self doesn't involve winning all the time. That simply isn't how life works. Almost inevitably, some things don't work out the way you planned; but that provides you an opportunity for recalibration, still working toward your best self. During chaos and failure, if you are doing the best you can with the resources available, be proud of your efforts and the way you show up; that is being your best.

Our brain controls everything we do, whether consciously or subconsciously. Let us choose the people, places, activities, and things that will enhance and support our efforts. Our time is important, and it is essential that we delegate it effectively and wisely. We need to have some "me time."

Cultivating self-forgiveness is a step in the right direction. We need to forgive ourselves for all negative experiences of the past. When you are on the journey of becoming the best version of yourself, you need to leave the negative past things behind, and the only way to do this is by forgiving yourself, and others. You deserve this. Our mind creates our reality, and if we really want to live our best life, we need to conquer our mind. We attract what we think. Start thinking positively, and let go of negativity.

I strongly recommend these exercises in improving your mindset.

- Practice gratitude.
- Stop complaining.
- Read more of what opens your mind.
- Bring clarity by redefining your goals.
- Fall in love with yourself. Celebrate yourself.
- Recognize that in all the great wide world, there is only one you. No one is you, and that is your superpower.

Once you identify the person you want to be, plan how to be that person. Start with the end in mind—your ideal self—and then take steps to get there. If you are feeling anxious about self-improvement, remember every person is completely unique, including you. Someone else's life path cannot be your benchmark of success. We all have different dreams, passions, and skills. There is no road map or ideal outcome in life, because everyone's path is theirs and theirs alone. Being the best version of yourself is about you—not other people. Transcend yourself!

With each goal achieved, you will get closer to being your best self. Each victory will confirm that you made a good choice in your goal and planning to improve your life. You will feel better about yourself with each accomplishment, finding it much easier to move to the next goal. Understanding our strengths and weaknesses in life helps us identify what we need to work on to live a more fulfilling life. The choice is ours!

Congratulations! You have decided you want to be your best self … Now what? What does it actually mean to be your best self? How will you know you are moving in the right direction? How will you know if something really is your best? There is no single formula or method when it comes to creating the absolute best self. It has been my experience that all humans are born with the ability to better themselves each and every day. Our ability to create the best version of ourselves starts at the same source, from within. Once we accept that we have the power to change ourselves, we are ready to start creating a successful, amazing us.

As we continue to work toward the PRC approach, we should all be well on our way to becoming our best self, as God intended! Identify the person you want to be. Now go forward confidently in the direction of your dreams. Live the life you imagine.

Here are a few motivational, inspirational nuggets in my reservoir that I feed on as needed.

- Pray often, and declutter regularly, mentally and emotionally.
- Before starting the day, tell yourself at least three things you are proud of. Let's start off our days celebrating ourselves.
- Be grateful for who you are; be grateful for who you are to become; be grateful for any boulder placed in your path. Use it as a stepping-stone.
- Meditate and be quiet. Just breathe. Deep breathing increases circulation by bringing oxygen to your muscles and brain, and it promotes a state of calmness.
- Believe in yourself, and manifest your vision, dreams, and goals to the Universe.
- Live intentionally; stay in the present.

Our ultimate goal in life is to become our best self, and our immediate goal is to recalibrate our path that will take us there. Keep in mind that you are not in competition with anyone, just simply striving to be better than you were yesterday! Whatever you are thinking, think bigger; invest in yourself. Keep doing your best, always striving to become a better version of yesterday's self. Your life is a reflection of your thoughts—change your thinking, change your life! Happiness is an inside job; don't assign anyone else that much power over your life. It all begins and ends in your mind. Whatever you give power to has power over ...
if you allow it. Do not be defined by your past experiences. You are capable of amazing things!

PERSEVERANCE, RESILIENCE & COURAGE WITH GRACE

Reflections

Was this chapter insightful or inspiring?

Your thoughts:

C O N C L U S I O N

Life can change forever in the blink of an eye; life changes for everyone.

You can have a better tomorrow if you believe you are the architect of your life.

This motivational manifesto nourishes a personal dialogue with highlighted experiences from my journey of trials and tribulations as I have traversed my highs and lows. I hope you have found inspiration in the many phrases, quotes, and scriptures that I frequently use throughout my life's path for encouragement. The pragmatic tips and suggestions, combined with some experiences I have encountered, may reflect exactly what you are experiencing, or someone else is experiencing, at this moment. Go ahead and make this an unexpectedly interesting read. Better yet, it is short and to the point.

It is intended to provide clarity, to keep you imagining and planning to become your best self and live your best life. Instead of allowing others' behavior to negatively shape your life, learn to grow and evolve from the experience. Be happy. Move on and trust those you can count on. I hope that this book has inspired and motivated you to set life goals, reflect on your past, and shape a future with purpose and intention.

PRC, I hope, provides reflections that will lead to personal insights while helping you view your life with perspective. Give yourself permission to live in a different manner, resulting in a positive, balance-filled life. Remember, you are the change you seek!

PERSEVERANCE, RESILIENCE, AND COURAGE GRATITUDE JOURNAL

Date:

Day 1:

Today, I am grateful for this:

_____

_____

_____

_____

_____

I am looking forward to achieving my planned goals in this way:

_____

_____

_____

_____

_____

I would describe the people who make my life exciting and make me laugh like this:

_____

_____

_____

_____

_____

_____

Today, I have accomplished this:

_____

_____

_____

_____

_____

_____

Be reminded that a grateful heart is a magnet for miracles. Manifest your vision and realize your dreams. Live the best life you deserve. Be happy!

Printed in the United States
by Baker & Taylor Publisher Services